NATIONAL GEOGRAPHIC
KiDS

ANIMAL GROUPS

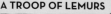
A TROOP OF LEMURS

NATIONAL
GEOGRAPHIC
KiDS

ANIMAL
GROUPS

JILL ESBAUM
PHOTOGRAPHS BY FRANS LANTING

NATIONAL GEOGRAPHIC
WASHINGTON, D.C.

From the jungles of the Amazon to the chilly icebergs of Antarctica and even in your own backyard, you'll find amazing animals. For many years, I have had the thrill of photographing elephants, butterflies, polar bears, and more. Sometimes I take pictures of the animals alone, but many times I spend time with animals in groups.

In this book, you'll discover that the name for a group of animals can be surprising. Some group names, like "herd," might sound familiar to you. Others, like a "cackle" of hyenas, might sound pretty funny. As you learn these different group names (and maybe laugh at a few of them), you'll also have a chance to take a close-up look at these incredible creatures. You'll learn some facts, too, about their habitats and behaviors as together we explore the far reaches of our planet.

Frans Lanting
Santa Cruz, California, 2015

A HUDDLE OF PENGUINS

Coalition

of Cheetahs

Wide-open savannas give cheetahs space to chase. Working in twos or threes, cheetahs quickly separate a weak wildebeest or gazelle from its fleeing herd. The prey is no match for these speedy hunters.

Celebration
of Polar Bears

Hungry polar bears lumber along, searching for seals by sniff-sniff-sniffing the frosty Arctic air. Furry feet keep them from slipping on snow and ice. Beneath their thick coats, black skin soaks up the sun's warmth.

Did you know?

- A polar bear's tongue is a dark, purplish blue.
- Polar bears can swim for up to a week without stopping.

Colony
of Atlantic Puffins

Puffins gather on seaside cliffs to hatch and raise their chicks, called pufflings. To feed them, parents dive for dinner, returning to their nesting burrows with fish-stuffed beaks. When they need to rest, they float on the waves.

Did **you** know?

- Puffins can swim underwater for up to a minute, flapping their wings to push themselves along.

- Beaks and feet fade to gray in winter, then turn bright orange in spring.

Raft

# of Sea Otters

The ocean is a perfect playground for sea otters, thanks to their cozy coats and paddle-shaped paws. Floating on their backs, they wobble with the waves as they clean their fur, munch lunch, or snuggle with their young.

Did you know?

- Every zebra's stripe pattern is different.
- Zebras keep friends looking neat by using their mouths to pull loose hair from one another's coats.

Zeal
of Zebras

Zebras snort when happy, greeting each other with ears up and faces reaching forward. But when a big cat, hyena, or crocodile nears, a zebra flattens its ears and pulls its head back. Loud whinnies warn friends. Luckily, one powerful kick can turn away a hungry lion.

Flight
of Monarch Butterflies

Flitting through sunshine, floating through shadows, this king of the butterflies flutters from flower to flower. At night, thousands cluster under leaves or branches. They hang upside down, wings folded, awaiting the warmth of the morning sun.

Did you know?

- Monarch babies, called larvae, eat nothing but leaves of the milkweed plant.

- Monarchs are the only butterflies that migrate, spending winter in parts of California and Mexico.

17

Cackle

of Hyenas

Hyenas seem to appear out of nowhere, silently sneaking up on supper. Females rule the group, keeping others in line with growls and grunts, squeals, whoops, and nervous "laughter."

Did you know?

- The hyena has the strongest jaws of any animal.

- A hyena eats every part of its prey, including bones, hooves, and teeth.

Troop
of Monkeys

Mona monkeys race from branch to branch, jumping and jabbering. These curious cuties are always on the lookout for a sweet bite of fruit—even when their cheek pouches are already stuffed! When danger nears, they freeze, silent and staring.

Did you know?

- Monas live in family groups of 40 to 50 monkeys.

- Everything they need is in trees—food, family, and cozy sleeping crannies—so they rarely come down to the ground.

# of Macaws

Bright splashes of color flash through canopy trees. Noisy squawks and screams let the whole neighborhood know who's coming—macaws! These flying rainbows live in rain forests, sometimes in groups of hundreds of birds.

23

Tower
of Giraffes

These graceful grazers wander the African savanna, nibbling sky-high acacia leaves. When they rest, they crowd close together to stay safe from lions.

Did **you** know?

- The heart of a giraffe weighs as much as a car tire.

- In a windstorm, a giraffe can close its nostrils to keep out the sand and dust.

ANIMAL FACTS

CHEETAH
GROUP: coalition
HOME: grassland
FOOD: hoofed animals
BABIES: one cub at a time

1

POLAR BEAR
GROUP: celebration, sleuth
HOME: sea ice
FOOD: seals
BABIES: one to three cubs at a time

2

PUFFIN
GROUP: colony
HOME: sky, sea, rocky cliffs
FOOD: small fish or eels
BABIES: one puffling at a time

3

SEA OTTER
GROUP: raft, romp
HOME: ocean
FOOD: clams, mussels, crabs, fish, octopuses
BABIES: one pup at a time

4

ZEBRA
GROUP: dazzle, zeal, herd, harem
HOME: grassland
FOOD: grasses
BABIES: one foal at a time

5

6 MONARCH BUTTERFLY
GROUP: flight, flutter
HOME: fields, meadows
FOOD: flower nectar
BABIES: eggs, up to 400–1,000 per female

7 SPOTTED HYENA
GROUP: cackle, clan
HOME: grassland, savanna, forest, mountains
FOOD: hoofed animals, birds, lizards, snakes
BABIES: two to four cubs at a time

8 MONA MONKEY
GROUP: troop
HOME: rain forest, woodland, swamps
FOOD: fruit, leaves, nuts, insects
BABIES: one infant at a time

9 MACAW
GROUP: flock, pandemonium
HOME: rain forest
FOOD: seeds, nuts, fruit, leaves, flowers
BABIES: one chick at a time

10 GIRAFFE
GROUP: tower, clan
HOME: grassland
FOOD: leaves
BABIES: one calf at a time

OTHER ANIMAL GROUPS

Most animal group names are **not** scientific or official. They are created by people like you and me who see a group of animals and **make up a name** that seems to fit. Some groups have been given **more than one name.** For example, somebody thought **"dazzle"** was a **good name** for a group of zebras, probably because those **bright stripes** dazzle our eyes. But they are also called a **"herd,"** which made more sense to somebody else. Here are some more animal group names. **Which ones do you think fit best?**

BATS.............................cloud, colony

BEARS...........................sleuth, sloth

BEETLES.......................aggregation, colony

CAMELS.........................caravan, train

CATS...........................pounce, clowder, glaring

CROCODILES...................bask, float

FLAMINGOES..................stand, flamboyance

FROGS..........................army, colony, forgery

GORILLAS......................band

GRASSHOPPERS.............cloud

HIPPOPOTAMUSES.......bloat

KANGAROOS..................mob, court, troop

LADYBUGS.....................loveliness

LEOPARDS.....................leap

LIZARDS.....................lounge

OWLS.....................stare, parliament

PANDAS.....................bamboo, cupboard

PARROTS.....................company, pandemonium

PENGUINS.....................colony, huddle

PORCUPINES.....................prickle

RHINOCEROSES.....................crash

SEALS.....................colony

SNAKES.....................nest, bed, pit, den, knot

SQUIRRELS.....................scurry, dray

STARFISH.....................constellation, galaxy

TIGERS.....................streak, ambush

WHALES.....................pod, gam

WHERE THE PICTURES WERE TAKEN

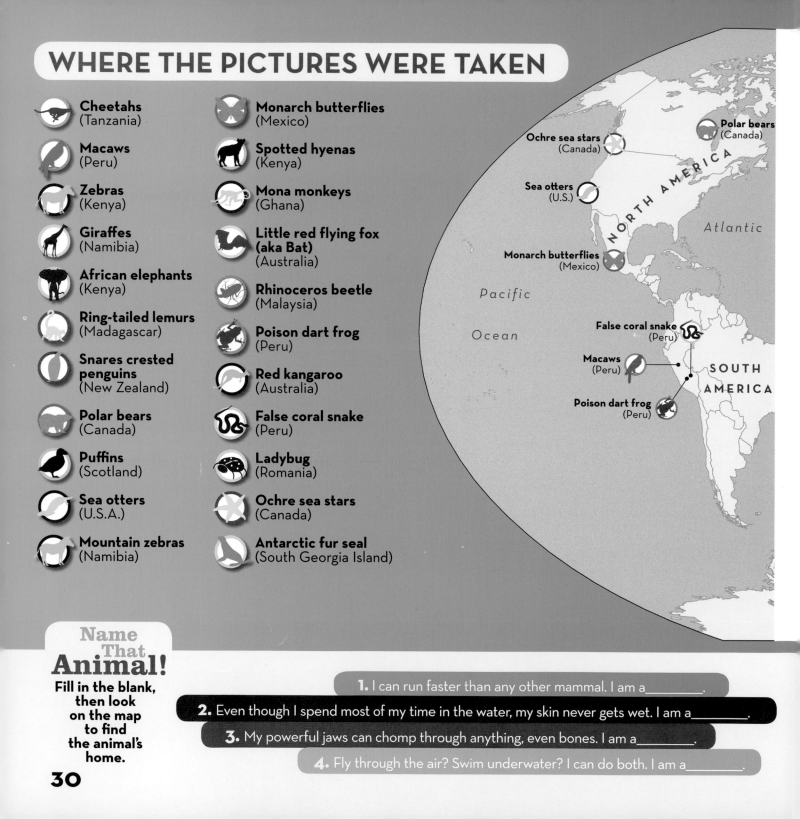

Cheetahs
(Tanzania)

Macaws
(Peru)

Zebras
(Kenya)

Giraffes
(Namibia)

African elephants
(Kenya)

Ring-tailed lemurs
(Madagascar)

Snares crested penguins
(New Zealand)

Polar bears
(Canada)

Puffins
(Scotland)

Sea otters
(U.S.A.)

Mountain zebras
(Namibia)

Monarch butterflies
(Mexico)

Spotted hyenas
(Kenya)

Mona monkeys
(Ghana)

Little red flying fox
(aka Bat)
(Australia)

Rhinoceros beetle
(Malaysia)

Poison dart frog
(Peru)

Red kangaroo
(Australia)

False coral snake
(Peru)

Ladybug
(Romania)

Ochre sea stars
(Canada)

Antarctic fur seal
(South Georgia Island)

Polar bears
(Canada)

Ochre sea stars
(Canada)

Sea otters
(U.S.)

Monarch butterflies
(Mexico)

Atlantic

NORTH AMERICA

Pacific

Ocean

False coral snake
(Peru)

Macaws
(Peru)

Poison dart frog
(Peru)

SOUTH
AMERICA

Name That Animal!

Fill in the blank, then look on the map to find the animal's home.

1. I can run faster than any other mammal. I am a _____.

2. Even though I spend most of my time in the water, my skin never gets wet. I am a _____.

3. My powerful jaws can chomp through anything, even bones. I am a _____.

4. Fly through the air? Swim underwater? I can do both. I am a _____.

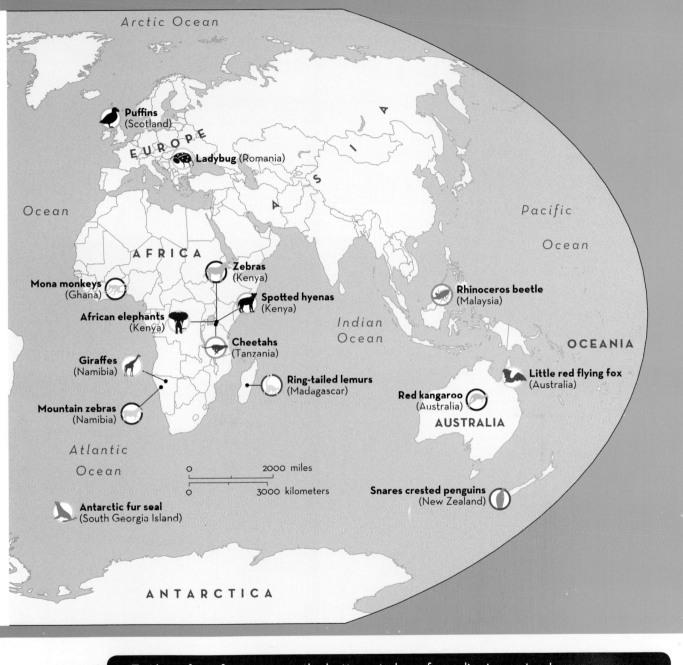

Arctic Ocean

Puffins
(Scotland)

EUROPE

Ladybug (Romania)

Ocean

ASIA

Pacific

Ocean

AFRICA

Zebras
(Kenya)

Mona monkeys
(Ghana)

Spotted hyenas
(Kenya)

Rhinoceros beetle
(Malaysia)

African elephants
(Kenya)

Indian
Ocean

OCEANIA

Cheetahs
(Tanzania)

Giraffes
(Namibia)

Ring-tailed lemurs
(Madagascar)

Little red flying fox
(Australia)

Red kangaroo
(Australia)

Mountain zebras
(Namibia)

AUSTRALIA

Atlantic

Ocean

0   2000 miles

0   3000 kilometers

Snares crested penguins
(New Zealand)

Antarctic fur seal
(South Georgia Island)

ANTARCTICA

5. I have furry feet—even on the bottom—to keep from slipping on ice. I am a_____.

6. I don't like to sleep alone. I'd rather hang with thousands of friends. I am a_____.

7. Everything I need can be found in trees. Come to the ground? No, thanks. I am a_____.

8. I can close my eyes and my nose to keep out swirling sand and dust. I am a_____.

Answers are on the following page.

GLOSSARY

CANOPY: the thick, leafy tops of tall rain forest trees

LARVAE: the tiny striped caterpillars that are freshly hatched monarch butterflies

MIGRATE: move from one region to another, usually for a season

SAVANNA: a grassy plain with few trees

WHINNIES: the gentle, neighing sounds made by zebras

ANSWERS: 1. cheetah 2. sea otter 3. spotted hyena 4. puffin 5. polar bear 6. monarch butterfly 7. mona monkey 8. giraffe

MORE INFORMATION

Not only is there some debate about what we should call certain animal groups, there are also differing opinions about how many animals make up a group. For this book, we're defining a group as three or more animals.

For more information about animals, check out these books and websites.

BOOKS

Domm, Kristin. *Atlantic Puffin: Little Brother of the North.* Halifax, Nova Scotia: Nimbus Publishing, 2007.

Hughes, Catherine D. *National Geographic Little Kids First Big Book of Animals.* Washington, D.C.: National Geographic, 2010.

Marsh, Laura. *National Geographic Readers: Cheetahs.* Washington, D.C.: National Geographic, 2011.

Marsh, Laura. *National Geographic Readers: Great Migrations: Butterflies.* Washington, D.C.: National Geographic, 2010.

Marsh, Laura. *National Geographic Readers: Polar Bears.* Washington, D.C.: National Geographic, 2013.

Marsh, Laura. *National Geographic Readers: Sea Otters.* Washington, D.C.: National Geographic, 2014.

WEBSITES

African Wildlife Foundation: awf.org/wildlife-conservation/all

Houston Zoo giraffe webcam: houstonzoo.org/meet-the-animals/giraffe-platform-cam/

National Geographic: kids.nationalgeographic.com/animals

Orangutan Foundation International: orangutan.org

San Diego Zoo: animals.sandiegozoo.org

Smithsonian National Zoological Park: nationalzoo.si.edu/animals

Photography by Frans Lanting; portrait of Jill Esbaum by Wiz of Oz Photography; photo of Frans Lanting by Christine Eckstrom

TO KYLIE —JILL ESBAUM

Text Copyright © 2015 Jill Esbaum
Photographs Copyright © 2015 Frans Lanting
Compilation Copyright © 2015 National Geographic Society

Staff for this book
Erica Green, Senior Editor
Julide Dengel, Art Director and Designer
David Seager, Designer
Jay Sumner, Photo Director
Carl Mehler, Director of Maps
Michael McNey and Sven M. Dolling, Map Research and Production
Paige Towler, Editorial Assistant
Allie Allen and Sanjida Rashid, Design Production Assistants
Michael Cassady, Photo Assistant
Grace Hill, Managing Editor
Joan Gossett, Senior Production Editor
Lewis R. Bassford, Production Manager
Darrick McRae, Manager, Production Services
Susan Borke, Legal and Business Affairs

Published by the National Geographic Society
Gary E. Knell, President and CEO
John M. Fahey, Chairman of the Board
Melina Gerosa Bellows, Chief Education Officer
Declan Moore, Chief Media Officer
Hector Sierra, Senior Vice President and General Manager, Book Division

Senior Management Team, Kids Publishing and Media
Nancy Laties Feresten, Senior Vice President; Jennifer Emmett, Vice President, Editorial Director, Kids Books; Julie Vosburgh Agnone, Vice President, Editorial Operations; Rachel Buchholz, Editor and Vice President, NG Kids magazine; Michelle Sullivan, Vice President, Kids Digital; Eva Absher-Schantz, Design Director; Jay Sumner, Photo Director; Hannah August, Marketing Director; R. Gary Colbert, Production Director

Digital Anne McCormack, Director; Laura Goertzel, Sara Zeglin, Producers; Jed Winer, Special Projects Assistant; Emma Rigney, Creative Producer; Brian Ford, Video Producer; Bianca Bowman, Assistant Producer; Natalie Jones, Senior Product Manager

National Geographic's net proceeds support vital exploration, conservation, research, and education programs.

For more information, please visit nationalgeographic.com, call 1-800-NGS LINE (647-5463), or write to the following address:
National Geographic Society
1145 17th Street N.W.
Washington, D.C. 20036-4688 U.S.A.

Visit us online at nationalgeographic.com/books

For librarians and teachers: ngchildrensbooks.org

More for kids from National Geographic: kids.nationalgeographic.com

For information about special discounts for bulk purchases, please contact National Geographic Books Special Sales: ngspecsales@ngs.org

For rights or permissions inquiries, please contact National Geographic Books Subsidiary Rights: ngbookrights@ngs.org

Hardcover ISBN: 978-1-4263-2060-6
Reinforced library binding ISBN: 978-1-4263-2061-3
Printed in Hong Kong
15/THK/1